Intermediate Piano Duet

We Wish You a Merry Christmas

ISBN 0-7935-9639-4

HAL•LEONARD®
CORPORATION
7777 W. BLUEMOUND RD. P.O. BOX 13819 MILWAUKEE, WI 53213

Visit Hal Leonard Online at
www.halleonard.com

We Wish You a
Merry Christmas

ANGELS WE HAVE HEARD ON HIGH

SECONDO

19th Century French Carol

Gently flowing

ANGELS WE HAVE HEARD ON HIGH

PRIMO

19th Century French Carol

Gently flowing

SECONDO

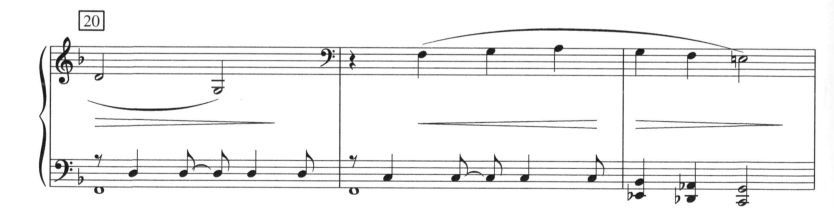

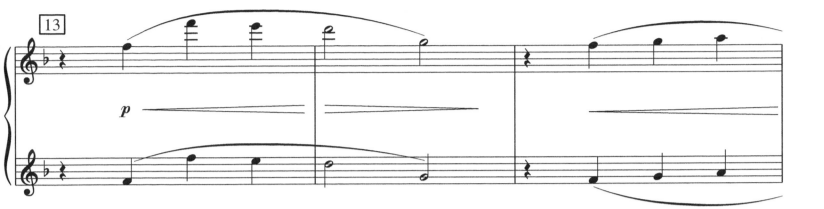

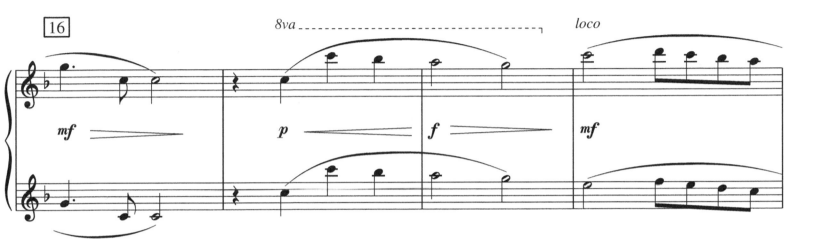

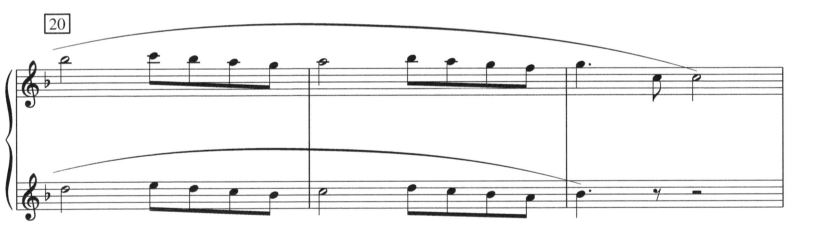

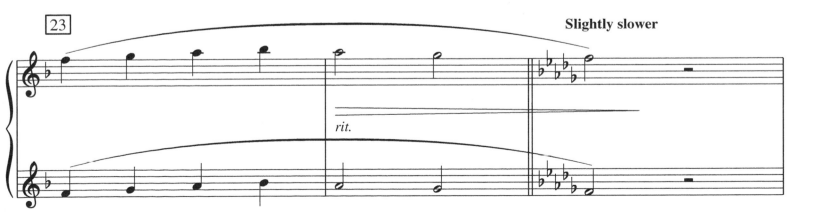

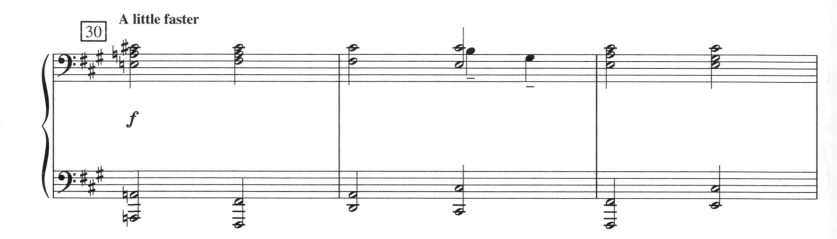

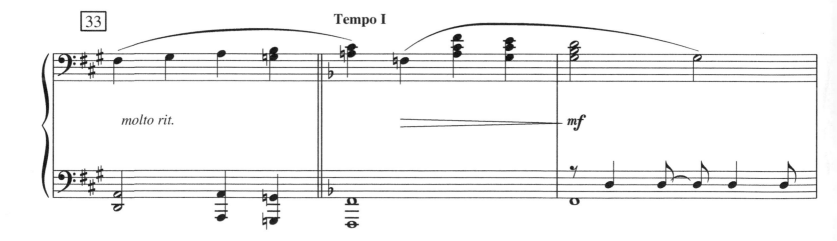

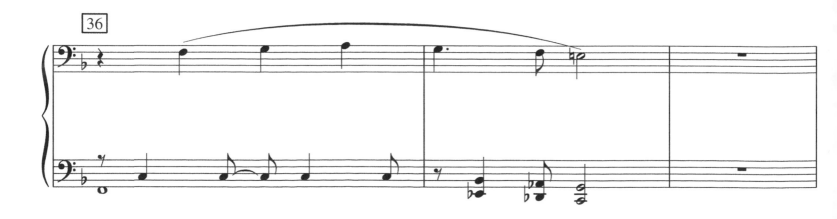

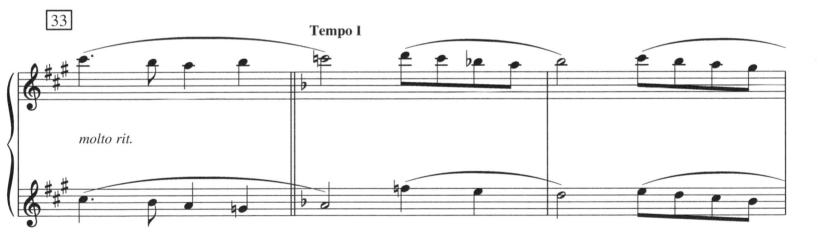

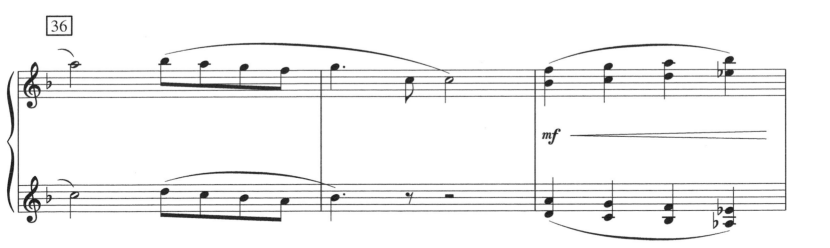

SECONDO

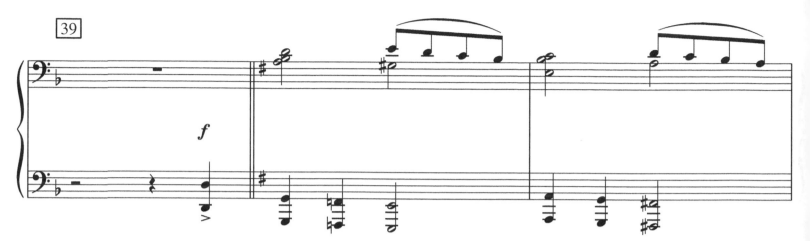

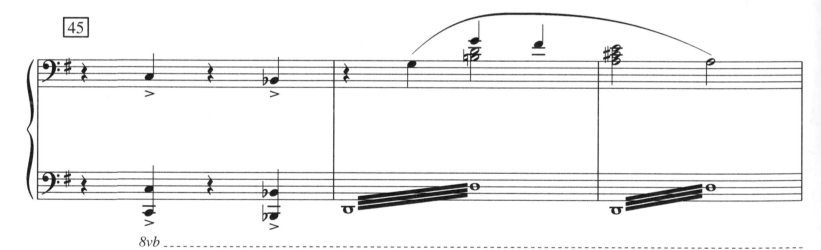

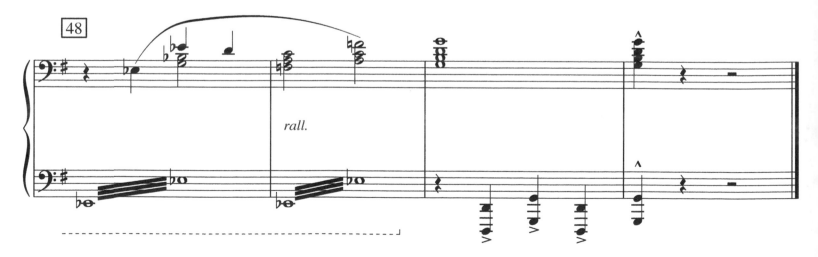

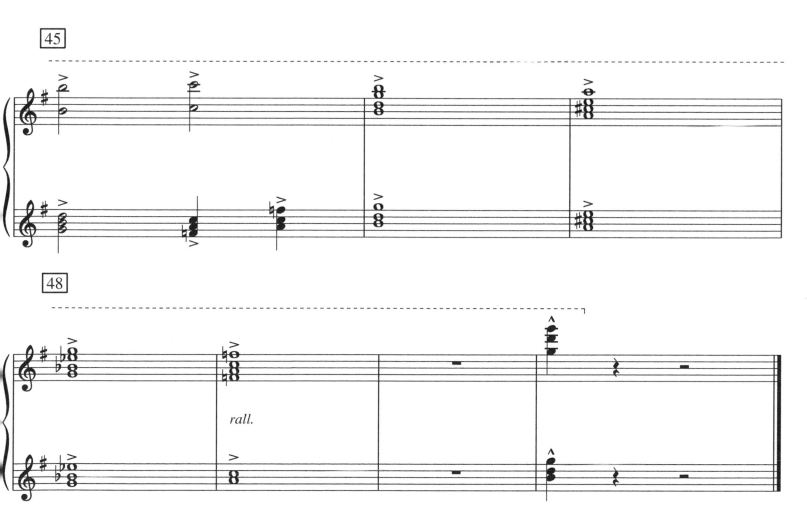

DECK THE HALL

SECONDO

Traditional Welsh Carol

Brightly

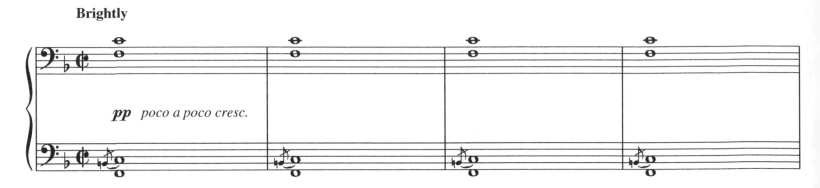

pp *poco a poco cresc.*

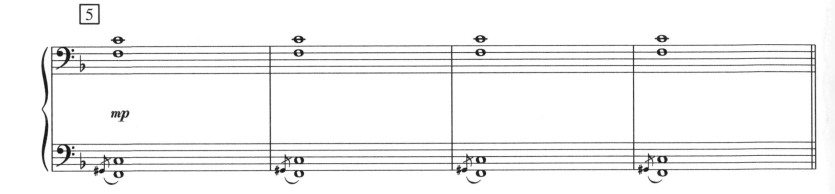

mp

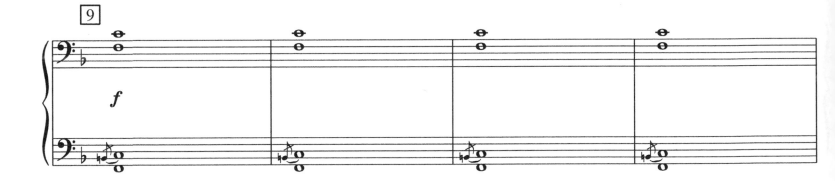

f

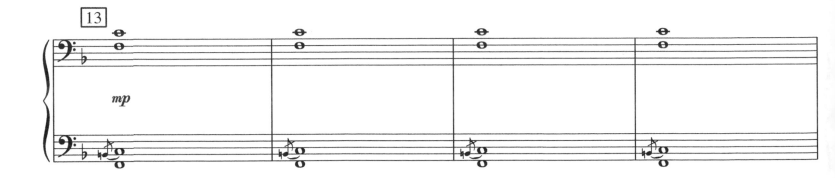

mp

DECK THE HALL

PRIMO

Traditional Welsh Carol

Brightly

SECONDO

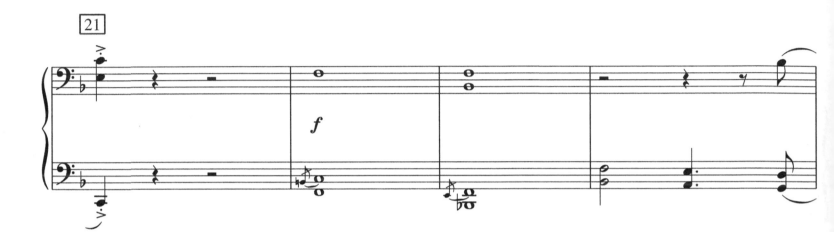

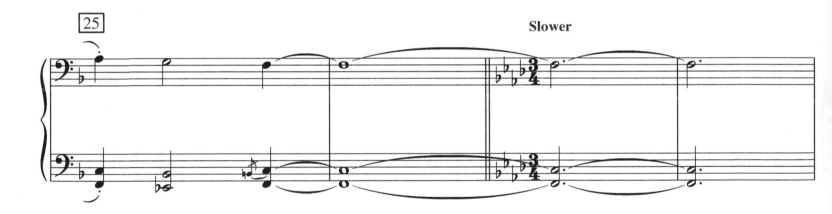

Slower

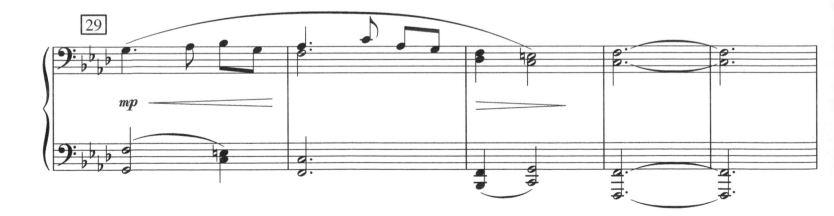

PRIMO

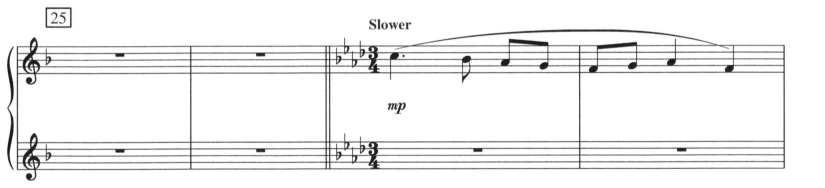

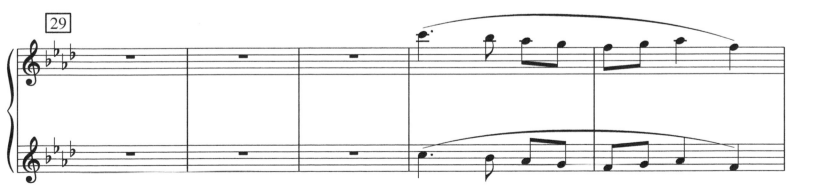

SECONDO

PRIMO

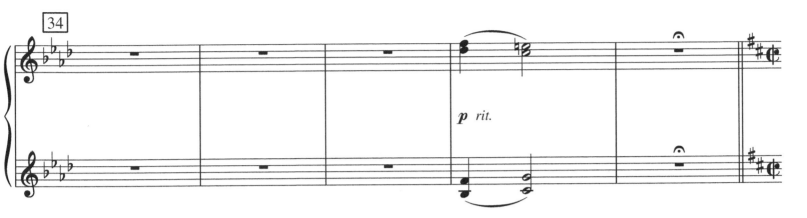

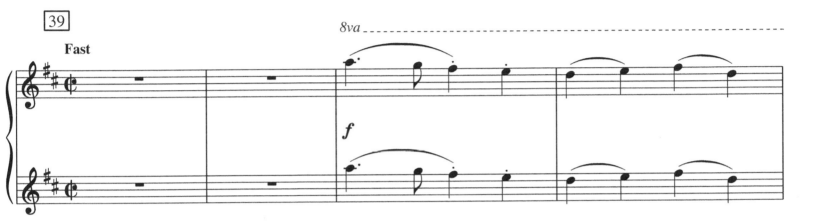

SECONDO

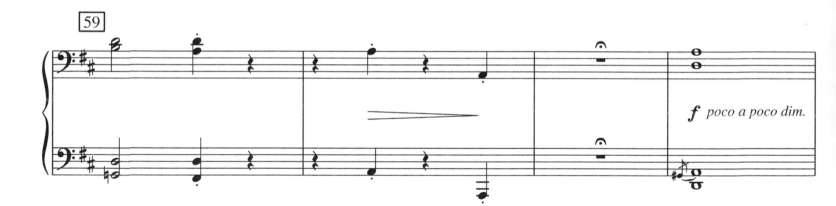

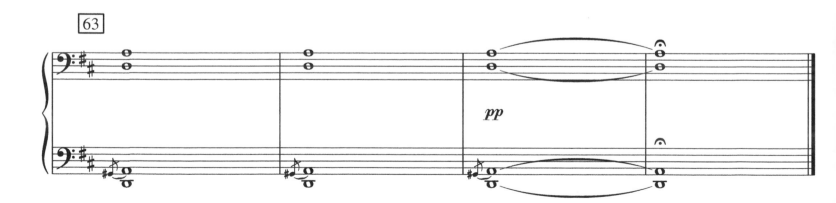

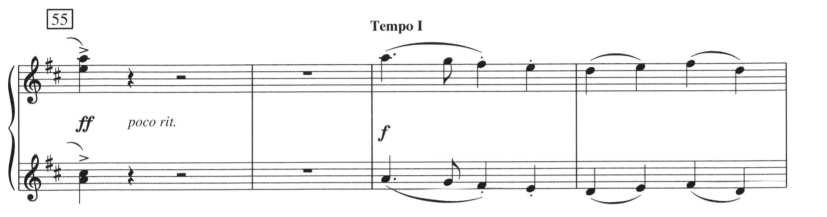

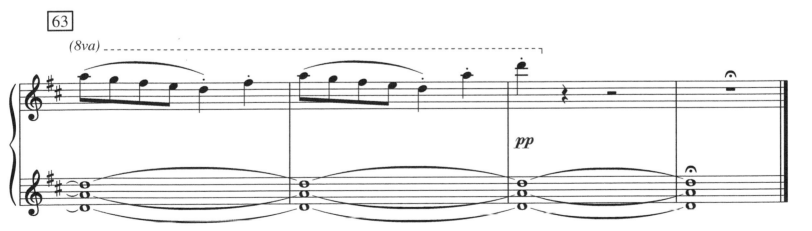

THE FIRST NOEL

SECONDO

17th Century English Carol

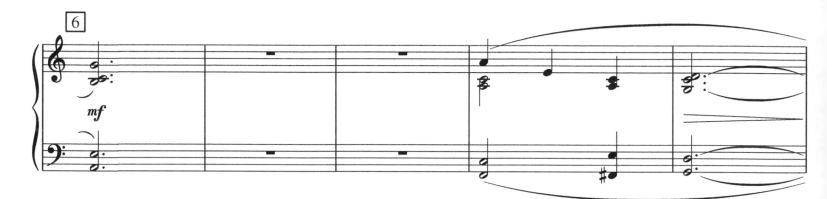

THE FIRST NOEL

PRIMO

17th Century English Carol

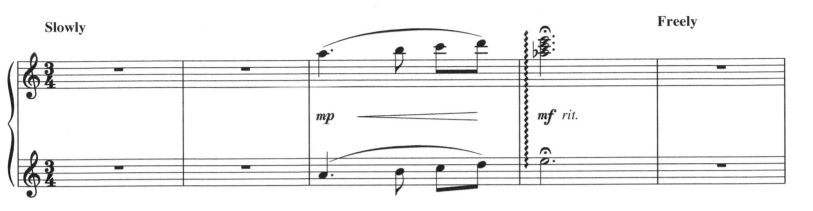

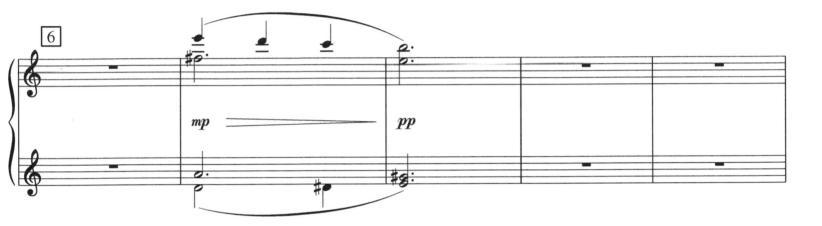

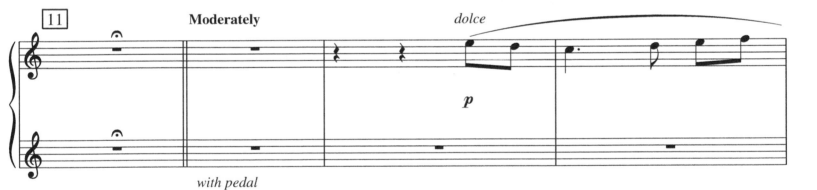

SECONDO

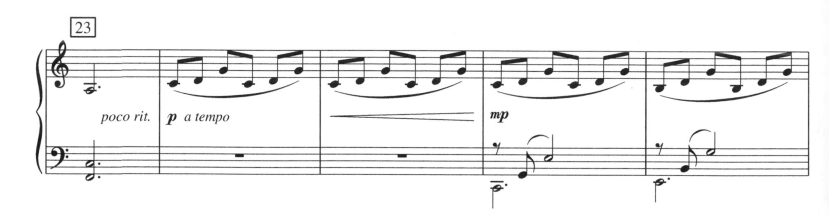

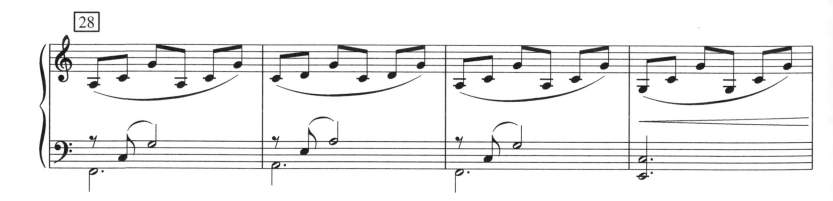

PRIMO

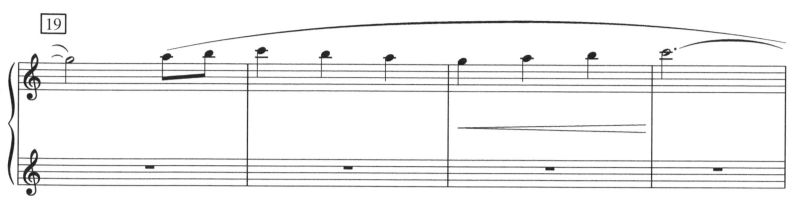

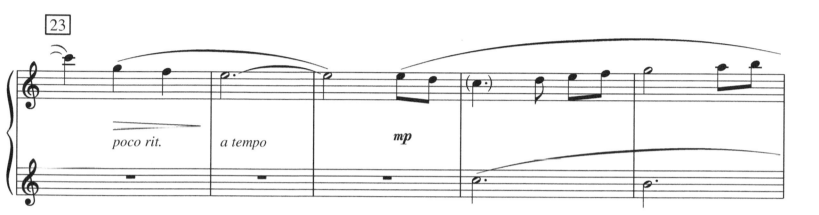

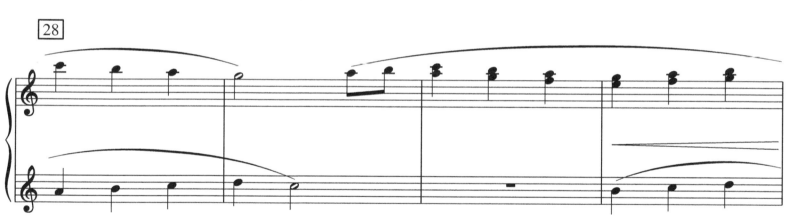

SECONDO

PRIMO

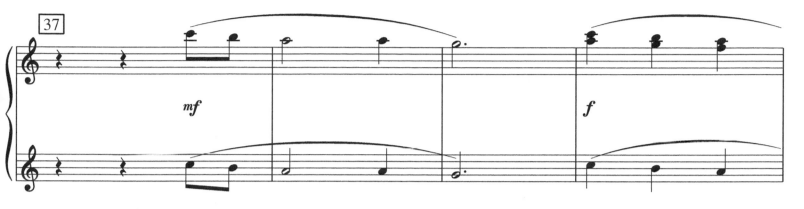

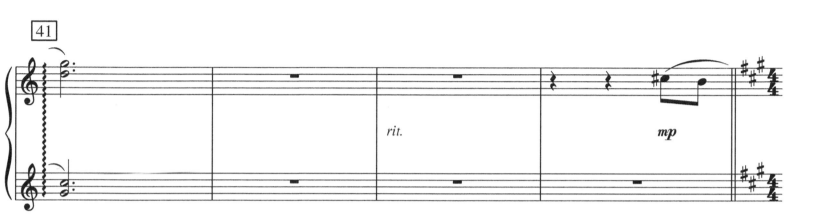

SECONDO

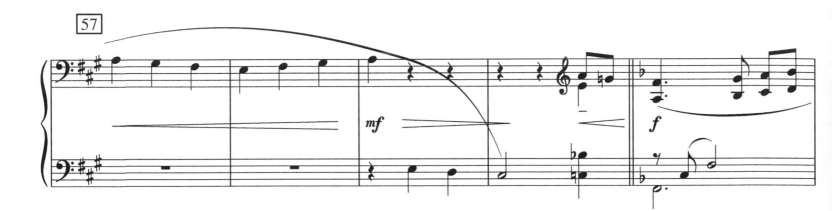

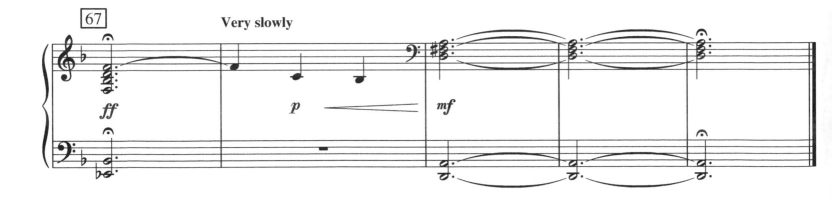

PRIMO

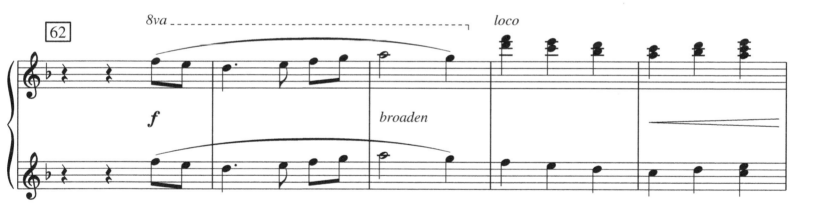

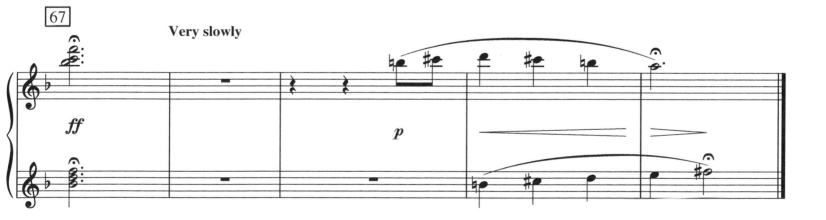

GOD REST YE MERRY, GENTLEMEN

SECONDO

19th Century English Carol

Sprightly

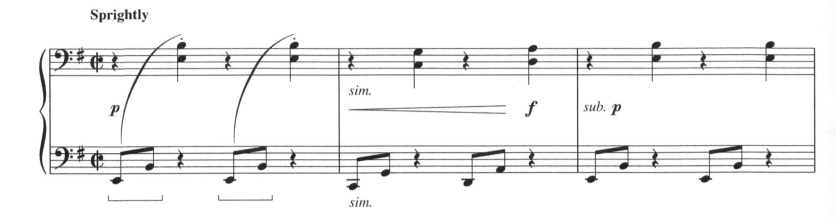

GOD REST YE MERRY, GENTLEMEN

PRIMO

19th Century English Carol

Sprightly

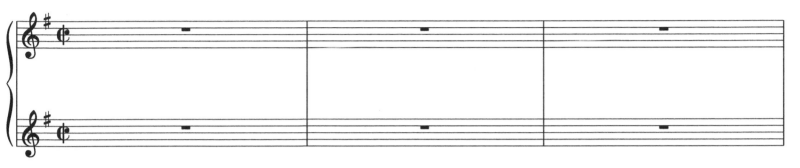

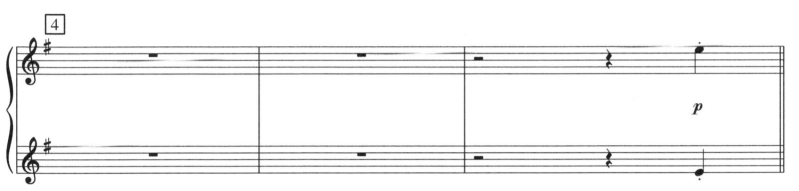

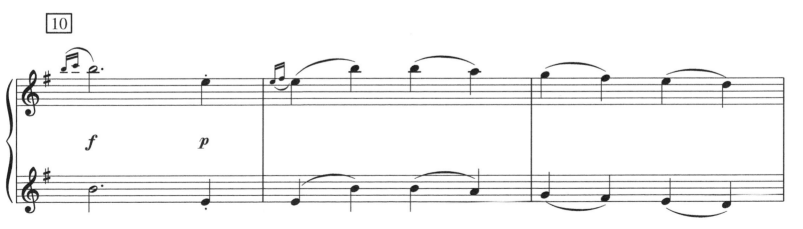

SECONDO

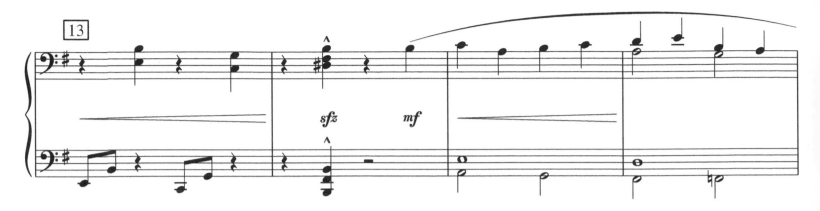

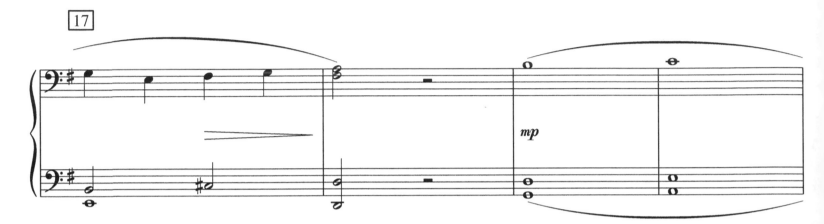

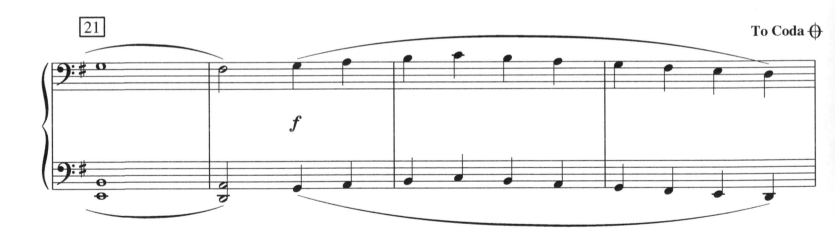

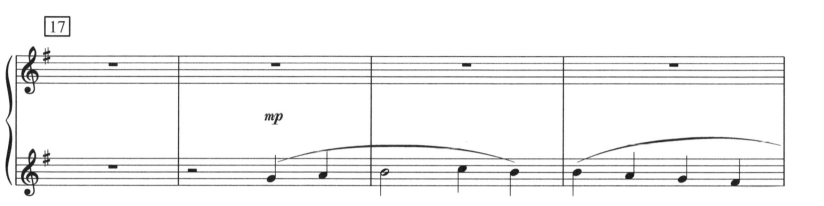

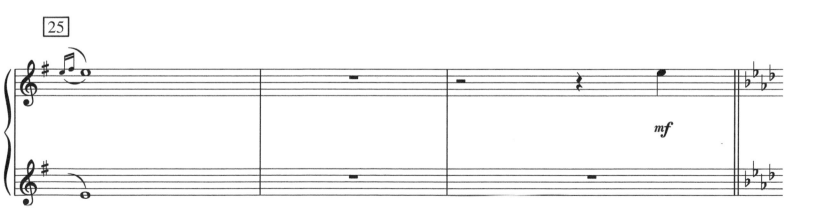

SECONDO

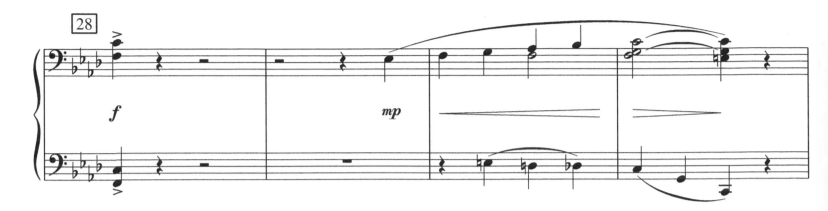

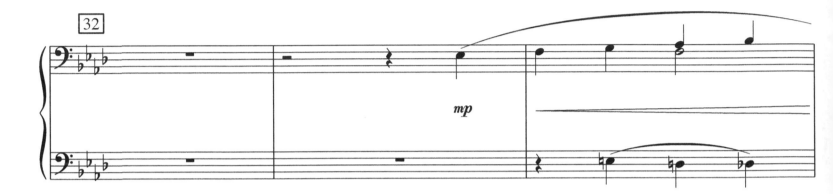

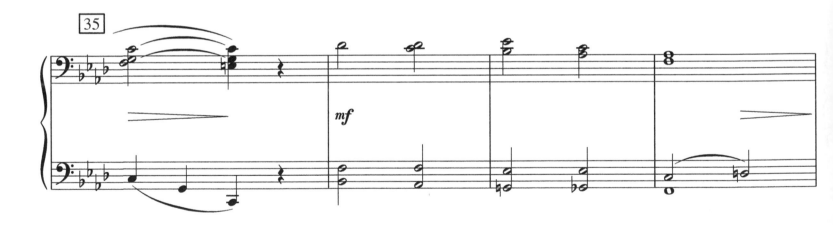

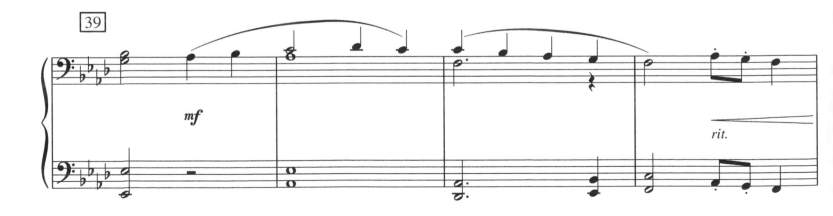

PRIMO

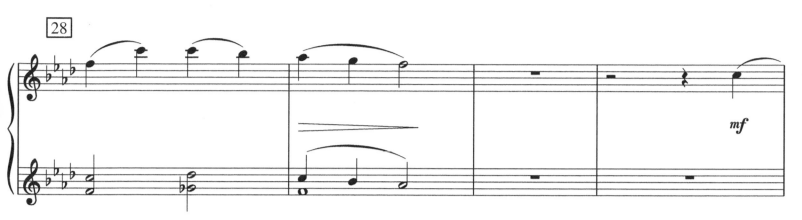

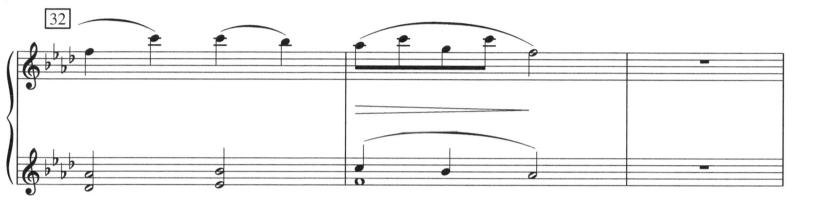

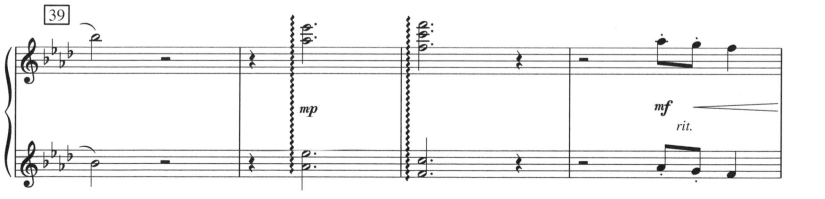

SECONDO

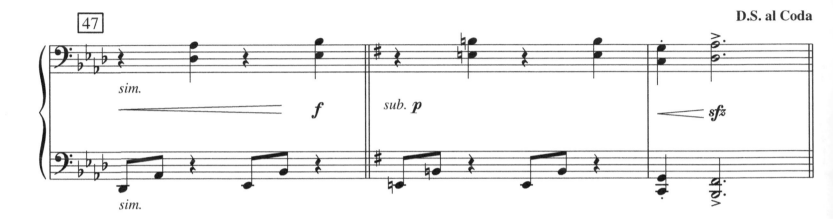

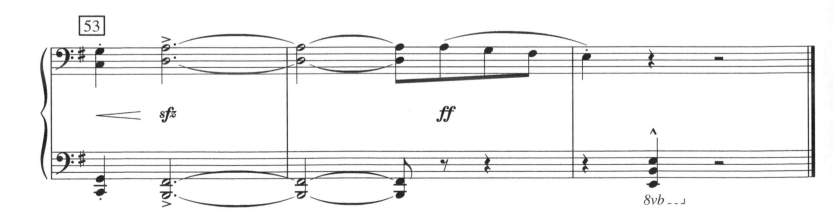

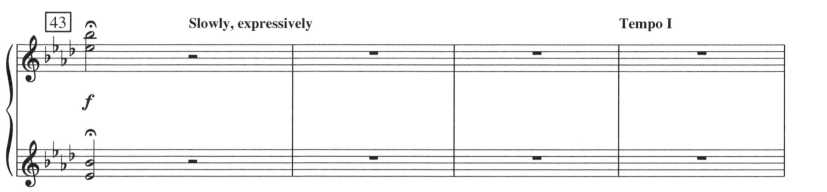

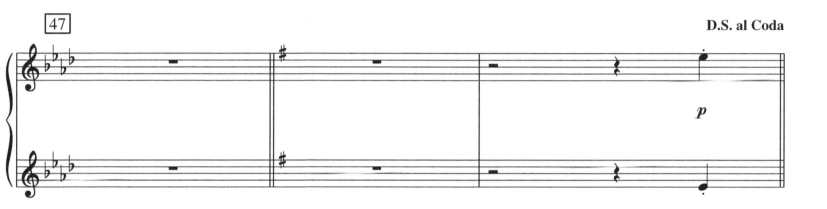

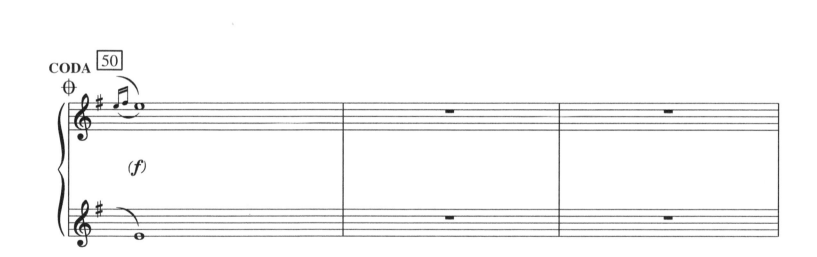

I HEARD THE BELLS ON CHRISTMAS DAY

SECONDO

Words by HENRY WADSWORTH LONGFELLOW
Music by JOHN BAPTISTE CALKIN

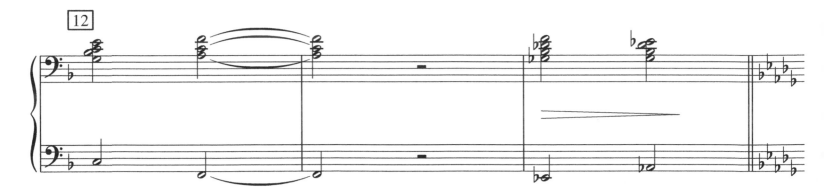

I HEARD THE BELLS ON CHRISTMAS DAY

PRIMO

Words by HENRY WADSWORTH LONGFELLOW
Music by JOHN BAPTISTE CALKIN

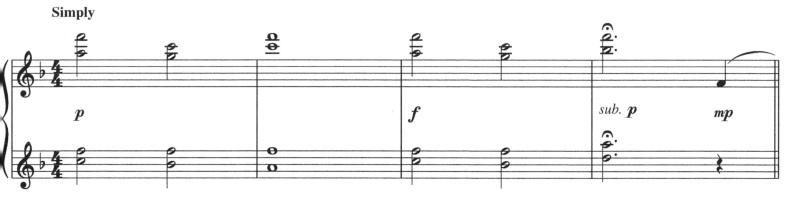

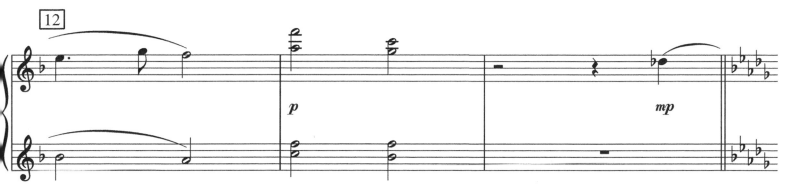

SECONDO

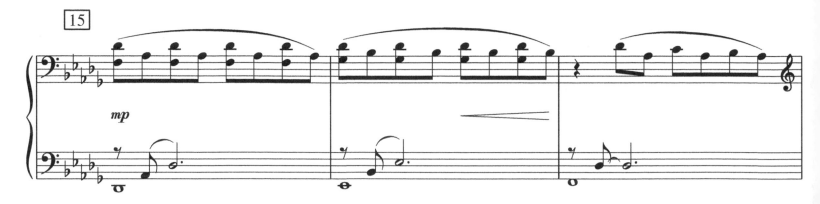

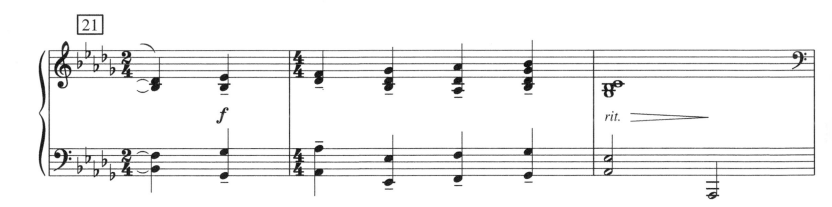

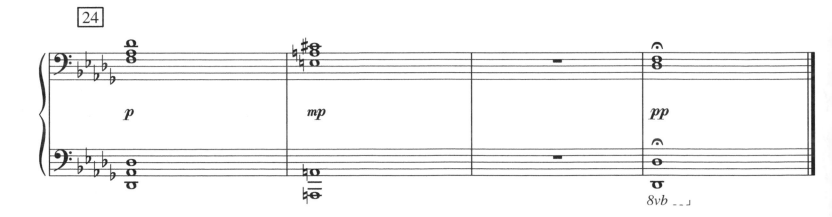

PRIMO

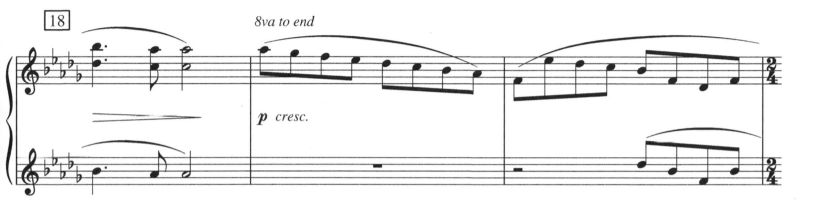

IT CAME UPON THE MIDNIGHT CLEAR

SECONDO

Words by EDMUND H. SEARS
Music by RICHARD STORRS WILLIS

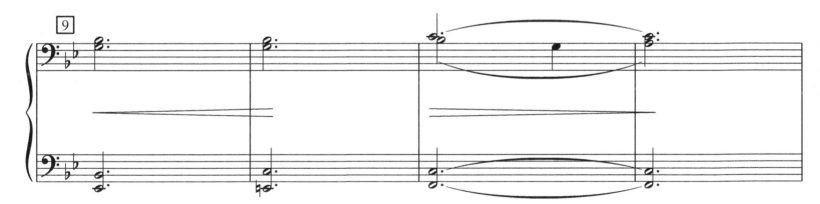

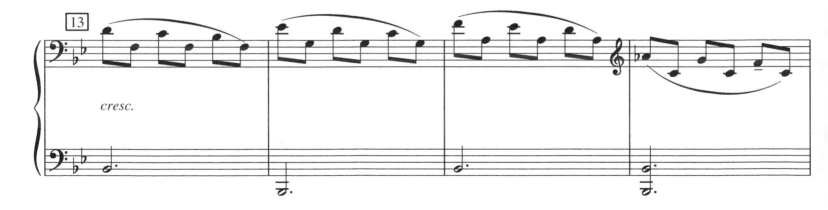

IT CAME UPON THE MIDNIGHT CLEAR

PRIMO

Words by EDMUND H. SEARS
Music by RICHARD STORRS WILLIS

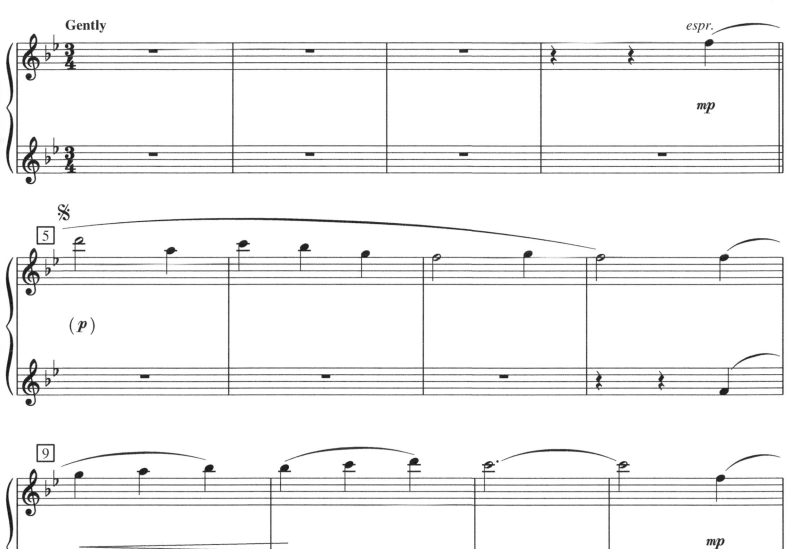

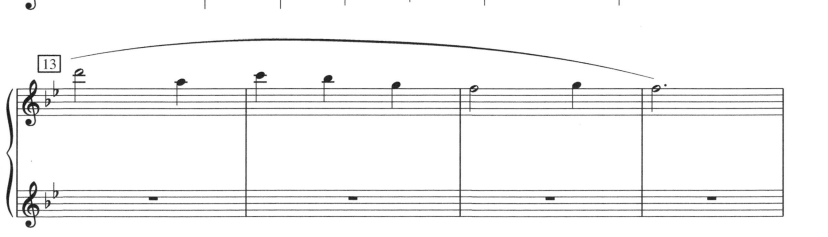

SECONDO

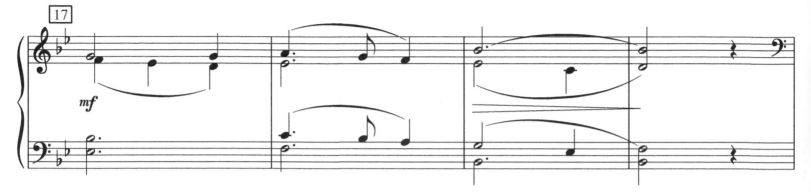

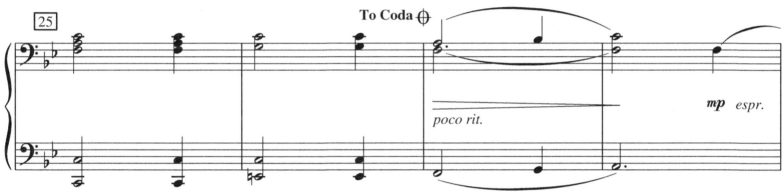

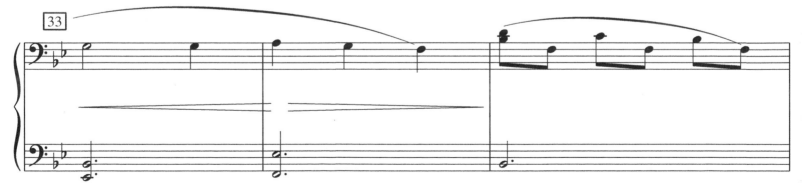

PRIMO

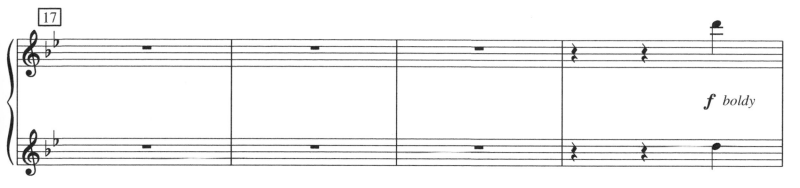

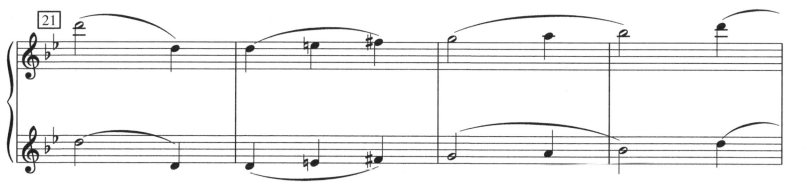

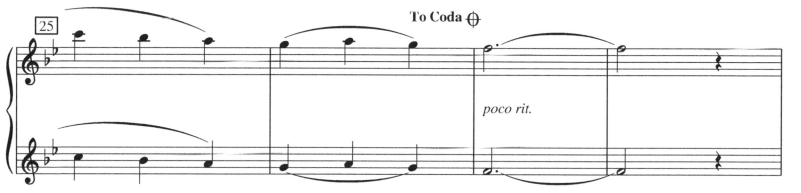

SECONDO

D.S. al Coda

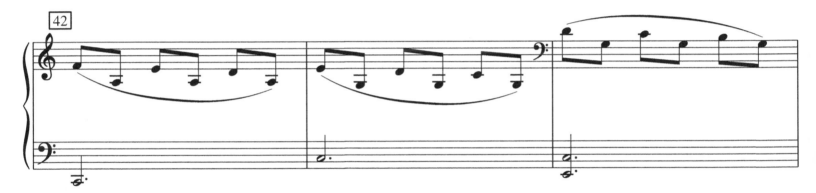

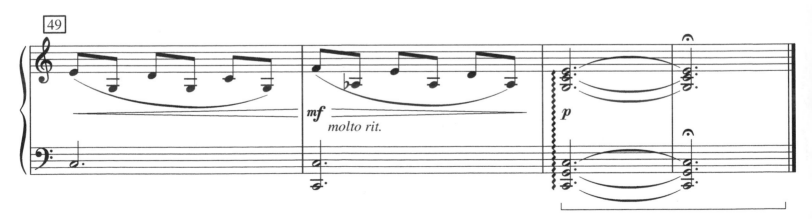

PRIMO

JINGLE BELLS

SECONDO

Words and Music by
J. PIERPONT

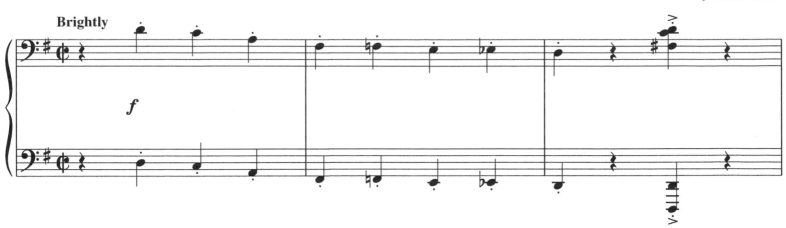

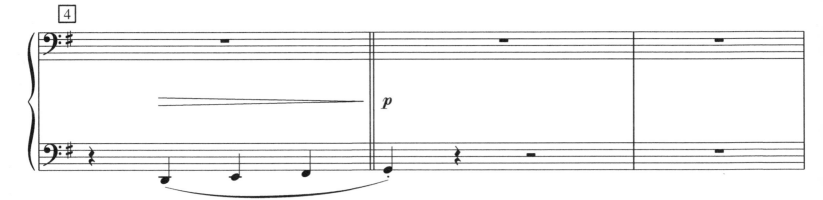

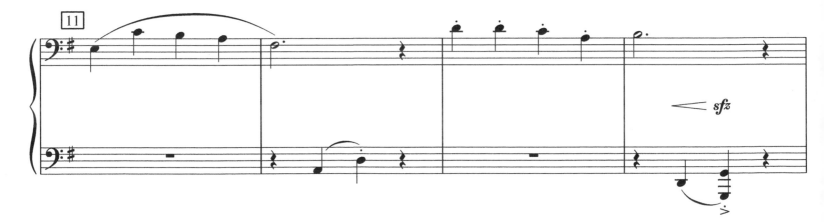

JINGLE BELLS

PRIMO

Words and Music by
J. PIERPONT

SECONDO

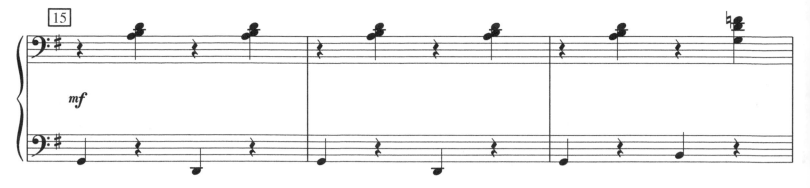

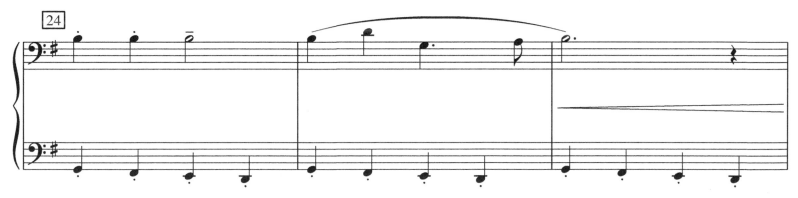

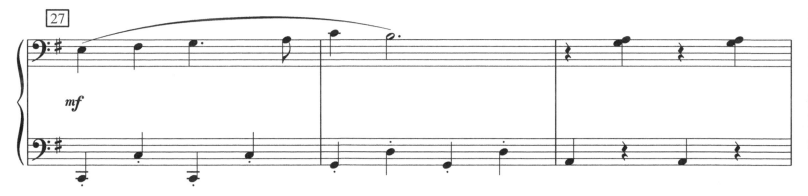

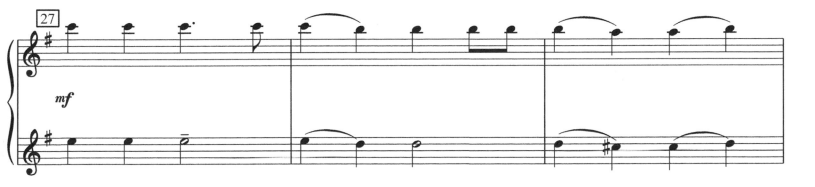

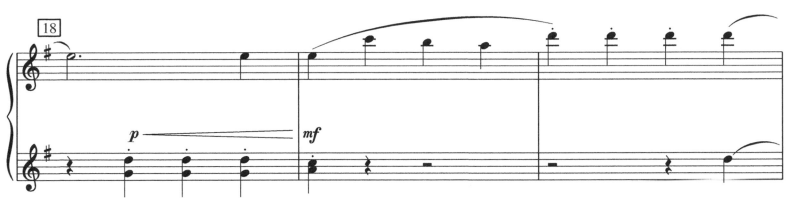

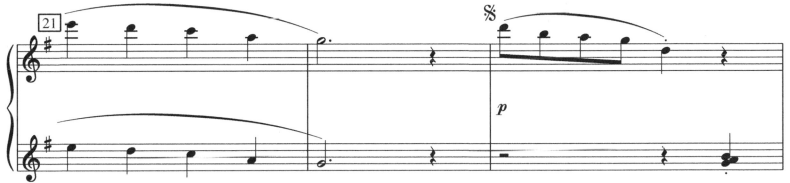

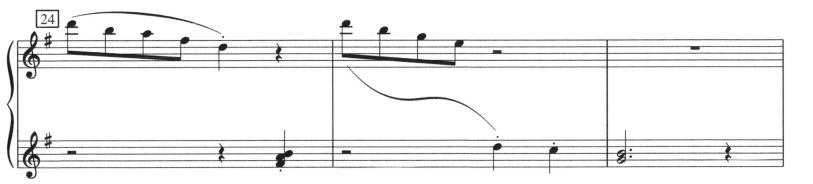

SECONDO

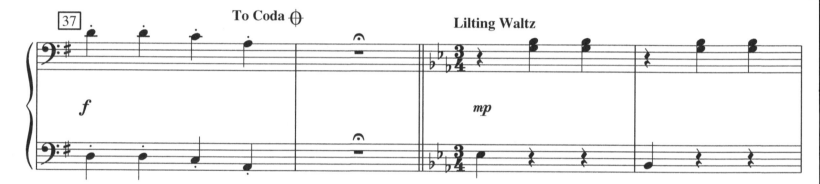

PRIMO

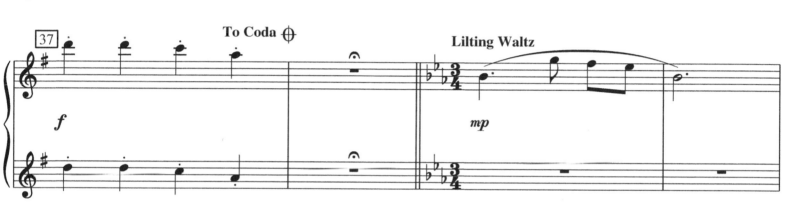

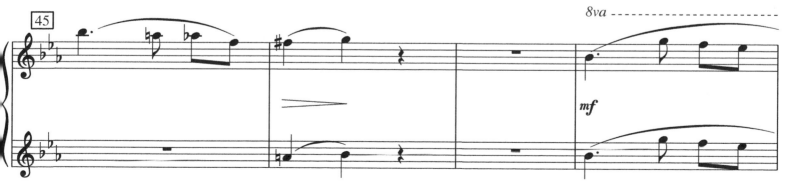

SECONDO

Tempo I   D.S. al Coda

CODA [57]

sub. **p**

[61]

poco a poco cresc.

ff

[65]

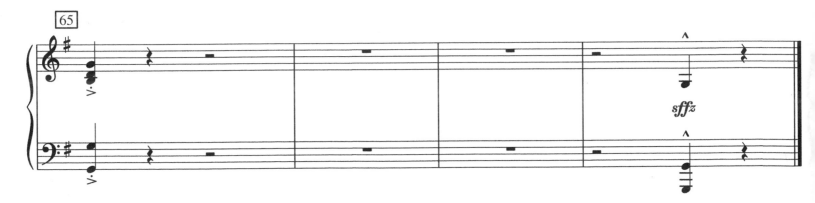

sffz

PRIMO

JOY TO THE WORLD

SECONDO

Words by ISAAC WATTS
Music by GEORGE F. HANDEL

With spirit

JOY TO THE WORLD

PRIMO

Words by ISAAC WATTS
Music by GEORGE F. HANDEL

With spirit

SECONDO

PRIMO

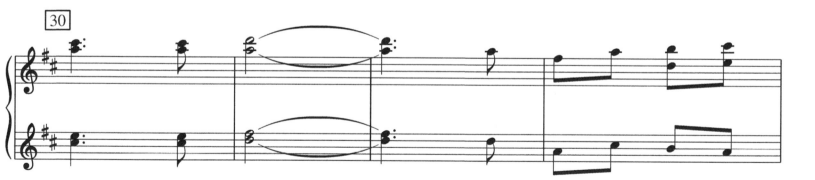

melody

58

PRIMO

38

42

(end melody)

47

51

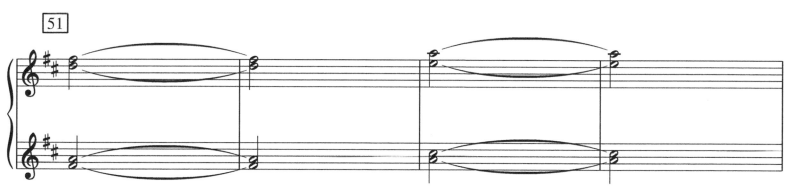

55

O LITTLE TOWN OF BETHLEHEM

SECONDO

Words by PHILLIPS BROOKS
Music by LEWIS H. REDNER

Moderately slow

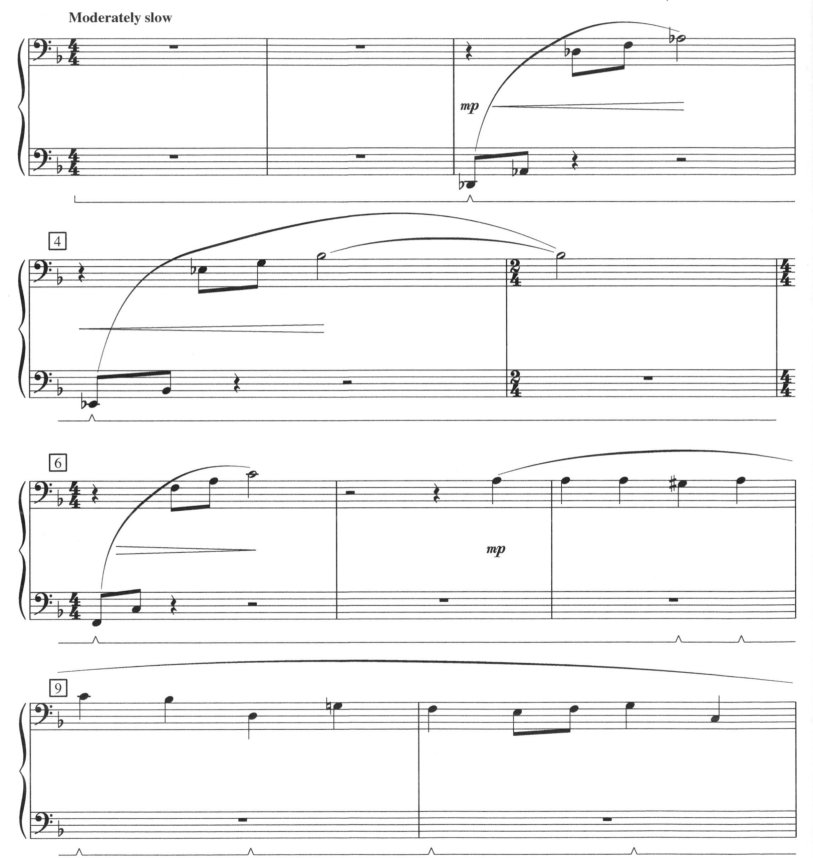

O LITTLE TOWN OF BETHLEHEM

PRIMO

Words by PHILLIPS BROOKS
Music by LEWIS H. REDNER

SECONDO

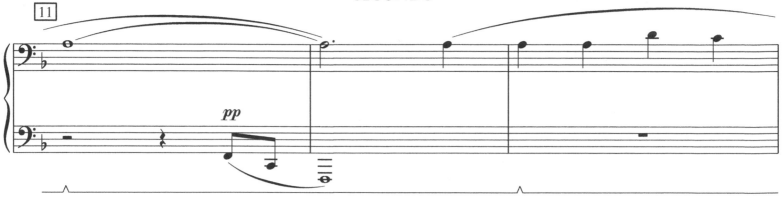

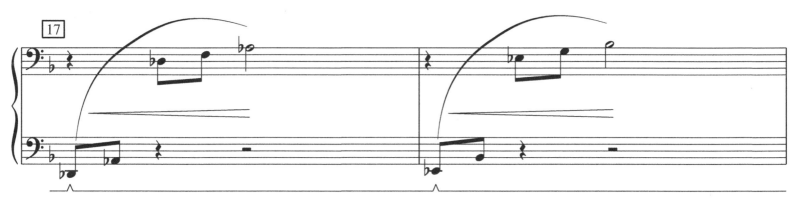

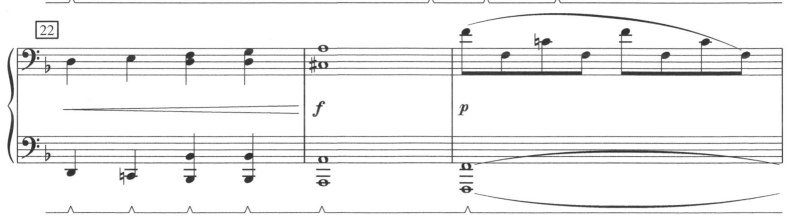

63

PRIMO

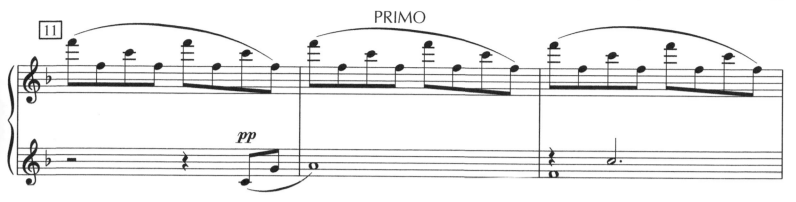

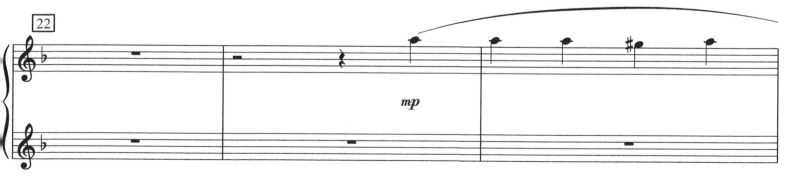

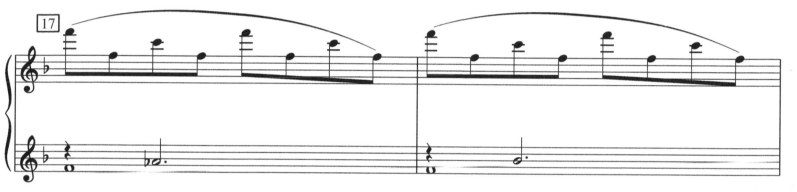

SECONDO

PRIMO

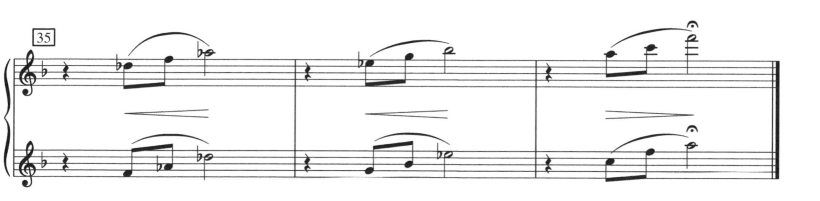

WE WISH YOU A MERRY CHRISTMAS

SECONDO

Traditional English Folksong

WE WISH YOU A MERRY CHRISTMAS

PRIMO

Traditional English Folksong

SECONDO

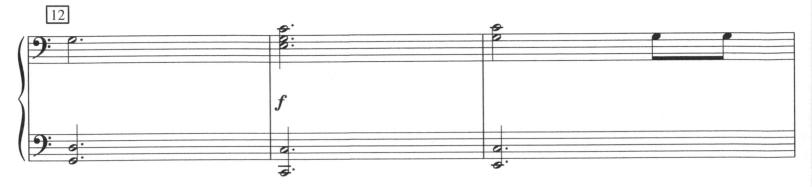

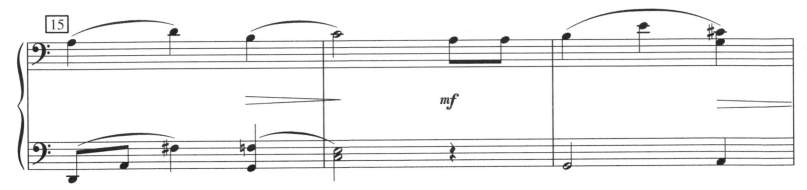

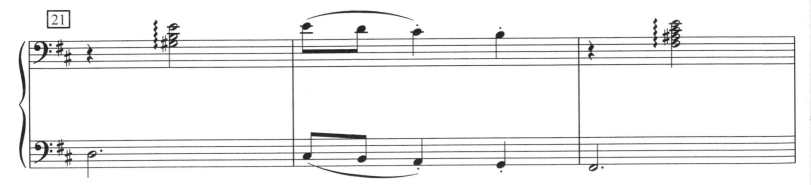

PRIMO

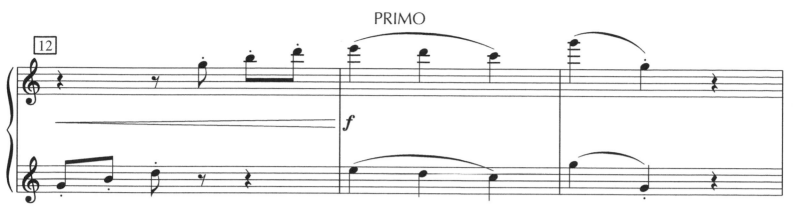

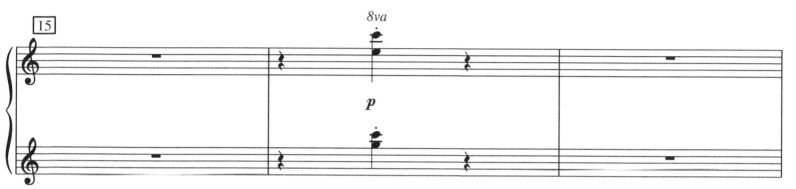

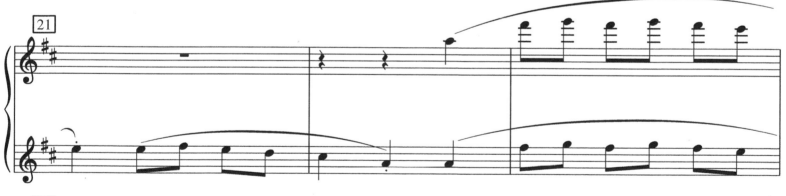

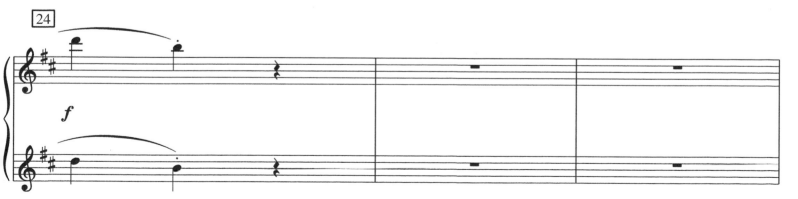

SECONDO

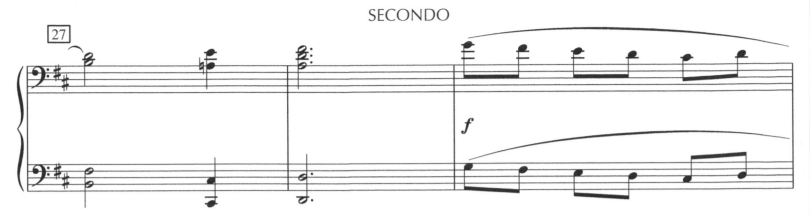

PRIMO

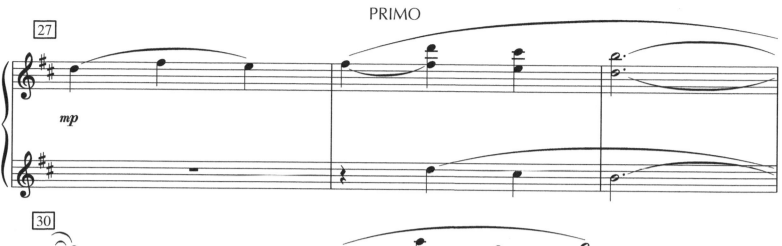

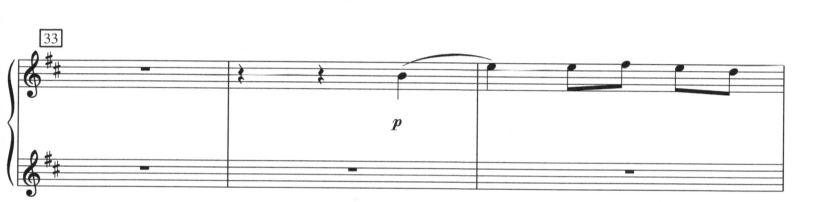

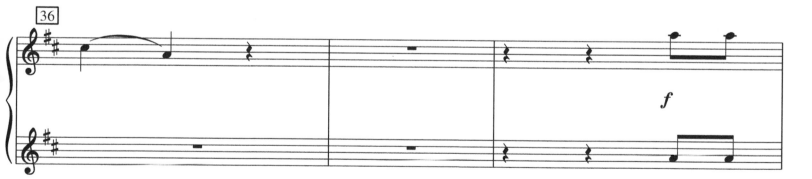

Piano For Two

A VARIETY OF PIANO DUETS FROM HAL LEONARD